Have Love

poems by

Deirdre Fagan

Finishing Line Press
Georgetown, Kentucky

Have Love

Copyright © 2019 by Deirdre Fagan
ISBN 978-1-64662-085-2 First Edition
All rights reserved under International and Pan-American Copyright Conventions. No part of this book may be reproduced in any manner whatsoever without written permission from the publisher, except in the case of brief quotations embodied in critical articles and reviews.

ACKNOWLEDGMENTS

"Knowledge" and "All the previous deaths were un-posted; word came by ring tone or Post, not post" in *Nine Muses Poetry*
"Outside In" in *Nine Muses Poetry* and was a Best of the Net Finalist, 2018
"Rose Colored Lovers" in *Poetry Quarterly*
"Father's Botany Lessons" in *Yellow Chair Review*
"Superstitions," in *Eunoia Review*
"No One Knew" and "Bartering in MI" in *The Opiate*
"Have Love" and "The Height of Gladness" in *Muddy River Poetry Review*
"The trouble with pairs" in *Ink, Sweat & Tears*
"X,Y,C" in *Eunoia Review*
"Night Terrors" in *The Blue Hour Magazine*
"While your husband is still able to stand" in *Poetry Breakfast*
"Going Hungry" in *Three Line Poetry*
"Most of the Days of the Week" and "Doorbell Advised" in *Melancholy Hyperbole*
"When a leaf blowing in the wind seems like a hello." in *Mused: Bella Online Literary Review*
"How Contentment Comes" in *Unbroken*
"Love Begets Love" in *The Literary Nest*
"Phantom Limbs" in *Boston Literary Magazine*
"Spilling Forth" in *Mothers Always Write*
"In Memoriam" in *Rat's Ass Review*

Publisher: Leah Maines
Editor: Christen Kincaid
Cover Art: Carrie Weis
Author Photo: Dave Robinson
Cover Design: Elizabeth Maines McCleavy

Printed in the USA on acid-free paper.
Order online: www.finishinglinepress.com
also available on amazon.com

Author inquiries and mail orders:
Finishing Line Press
P. O. Box 1626
Georgetown, Kentucky 40324
U. S. A.

Table of Contents

Knowledge 1

Rose Colored Lovers 2

Father's Botany Lessons 3

Superstitions 4

No One Knew 5

Have Love 8

The Trouble with Pairs 9

X, Y, C 10

Night Terrors 12

While Your Husband Is Still Able to Stand 13

All the Previous Deaths Were Un-Posted; Word Came By
    Ring Tone Or Post, Not Post 14

Going Hungry 15

Most of the Days of the Week 16

When a Leaf Blowing in the Wind Seems like a Hello 18

How Contentment Comes 19

Bartering In MI 20

Love Begets Love 21

Outside In 23

Doorbell Advised 24

The Height Of Gladness 26

Phantom Limbs 27

Spilling Forth 28

In Memoriam 29

Author's Note 30

For my lovely husband, Dave, my very missed late husband, Bob, and our remarkable children, Liam and Maeve, without whom this book would not have been birthed.

Knowledge

Mostly we are unaware
of ourselves

We fumble familiarly
our minds navigating their spaces
our bodies rounding corners
absently avoiding debris

Upon extending an arm
at the right height
of a doorknob
while staring ahead
without blinking

we enter our bedrooms
where we are suddenly surprised
by the faint recognition
of our own
scents

Rose Colored Lovers

I eyed what I thought was a tomato
on a rose bush and reflected,
which is more succulent?

One makes lovers, the other sates,
but which nourishes?

I would like to live on roses, each petal's dew
cascading over my tongue as guileless as a cherry tomato's,
skin punctured tenderly,
penetration barely delectable.

Father's Botany Lessons

"Purple loosestrife," you said as you drove

The opera blared on the public radio station
while I sat consumed in thought

I recalled your having pointed that out
the day before, on our way for ice cream

"It chokes out everything around it," you said.
"Huh," I said.

We spent hours that summer driving to town for
household goods, food, odds and ends

"Purple loosestrife," you'd regularly announce with everything
from recognition to a bellow to a hushed whisper

"It chokes everything around it out," you'd say, pointing,
the repetition of your line becoming a chorus of country curves

You tried to talk me out of it: "You don't have to do this,"
you whispered in my ear as you walked me down the aisle that June

It was the summer of lessons in botany,
or relationships, perhaps.

I still wonder which as I educate the children I chose to have
about the weed

"It chokes out everything around it," I inform them, remembering its
radiant color and yours, and wondering what I mean, what you meant

Superstitions

We believe
if we say a thing
we risk it becoming true

like when we say
"I haven't gotten sick yet—
knock on wood."

We do the same with
I love you

No One Knew

I.

No one knew when I met a boy over a bong
on New Year's Eve, months after my mother
died, and before my story reached my lips,
that it was the untelling of childhood
that drove me to him.

A boy without a driver's license,
without I.D., without a checkbook,
into his arms and waterbed I came.

I don't have to tell you
he wasn't the first.

II.

The first engagement happened
on one knee in a restaurant,
but my mother's cancer
grew in the desert, and that boy
was all water, and the sand
knew.

Mother was dying
and the boy of my youth was driving cattle
while the dust devils enveloped my heart,
so he drove me too.

Sometimes it is the past that beckons the firsts to your bed.

Each boy broken off can put a piece of you together.

III.

One engagement, one divorce, two rings in the tree now.

IV.

The second marriage was clever and kind, the first boy
to hear of the untold man of my childhood.

He loved me anyway.

V.

But there is a kind of love that brings more love.

It welcomes in the dark and the light with heart, mind, and arms,
tongues, the eyes seeing each other and oneself reflected at once.

This love is the one that brought forth two beauties,
shining, whole, unharmed, as yet untouched.

Our beloved was taken, but our love still grows.

IV.

Four rings total in the tree; four rings removed from the finger.

One more ring.

V.

The fourth and the fifth rings are the hardest to tell apart.

They are both beautiful.

They share the same stone.

VI.

No one knows the journey.

The untelling of a childhood sometimes dooms us to repeat it,
the first one we tell may not always be the one that sticks,
the best one to stick may not always be undone by the past, and
another marriage is not always a curse. It is often a blessing.

Each marriage scroll rolls and unrolls a newer older you.

VII.

There are others like you who fold origami-like
into the animals they become through the glee
that turns into the hardship that shakes them free.

I've met them. I will tell you.

Have Love

We don't have to mate for life to
make love.

And by make, I mean give,
I mean have,
love.

I had love before you.

But in the period of giving love,
we give something to ourselves.

Something like this smoothed,
shiny stone that no longer has
rough edges but can
still
sink.

Some was not love.

The trouble with pairs

I want to be inside of you
No, not like that

I want to unzip you
And climb inside

Big toe first, then
a dipping of my head

Until I'm fully upright
and enclosed in your dark

Your sinews and synapses
making room for all of me

I don't want to meet
where lips meet, anymore

Or where parts may be
joined, but inevitably part

I want to get inside so far
there is no getting out

Where two truly are one
and departure becomes impossible

Close is never close enough

And isn't that the trouble with
pairs?

X, Y, C

In the dead of night I reach for your hand beneath mounds of covers, my breath almost visible in the winter's cold.

I stroke your wedding band, a circle of platinum, securely rubbing its cool metal, fully aware of the distance between its arrival and now.

A warm southern breeze sweeps over me as I lay my hand over yours and take in the rhythms of your breath.

Wiggling my toes in remembered sand, I succumb to memory as your inhales and exhales recall the crashing waves of vows which transported us from surfside to this inside, here.

An ivory dress, a crisp suit, bare feet, the horizon, lifted chins, the absence of time or future.

We were thinner then, unweighted by a life which neither of us was even half-aware had a distance so fleeting no memory would be long enough or deep enough to narrow.

My ankle reaches for yours. Draping my leg across the inches that separate, I longingly navigate the covers with my toes, seeking the warmth and softness of the top of your foot.

My ankle descends, and for a moment, there is contact. Arm still reaching, hand atop hand, I am part X, part Y as I splay hand and foot, effortlessly longing to return you to my seaside if only for a moment.

There is a grumble, an arch, a pivot, a rolling away, a deep sleep exhale.

And then a back.

Abandoned, left upward facing and sprawled, I am jarred from memory back into winter.

Receding into a C, I am nearly at the beginning again, conserving the warmth of my own body, receding in my mind to a future when my reach will be unmet by your warmth, not by a turned back but by the absence of one.

Your ring will be in a memory chest, your soft feet sanded away, your breath with my memories of waves crashing. Or, my ring, my feet, my breath.

Aghast at this sudden vision of everlasting winter, I inch my full body in your direction, seeking the fullest body warmth—belly to back, knee to back of knee, lips to back of neck—which consoles, if

only
temporarily.

Night Terrors
For D.S.

Don Quixote tilted at windmills
Alice fell down the rabbit hole
shouting from a well bottom
is seldom heard when the
moon's rays beam on

Fissures come without warning as
darkness consumes the wide-eyed
swords are feebly brandished
the earth's swallows are whole

When night comes
seldom or in repeat
it is not with one foot we slip
but with two
neither of which acts as a guide

The wounds received in battle bestow honor
they do not take it away
but Alice must run as fast as she can
just to stay in one piece.

While your husband is still able to stand

you fasten the tabs
by reaching around from behind,
and your wrist is tickled by his hairy
middle, while you lean in, close your
eyes, and pause to smell the skin on his back.

when your husband tells you to call
what he's been wearing diapers
because that's what they are,
you do.

his head lowers as you finish the job.

When you get groceries, he encourages you to
take your time, enjoy being without him,
not to rush home, he is clean. He will be fine.

no matter how many times you tell
him it doesn't matter to you,
you will be unable to unburden him.

upon learning, as you set down the groceries,
he has called an aid, instead of you,
a gift to you, the way he used to do
the vacuuming, or bring you flowers,
your own head will lower.

you will place the ice-cold coffee you have
brought him beside his chair and thank him
for being alive.

All the previous deaths were un-posted; word came by ring tone or Post, not post.

The first death by email was Linda's,
the stunned silence of a monitor, your face.

You raced down the hall and leapt,
shrieking to your then-well husband, "Linda is dead!"

You have since committed the crime of alerting,
signaling death's sentinel by a mouse-click of Send.

When your husband died, you kept him home one more night,
the urgency of a funeral home, a coroner, not your own.

You slept on the futon beside the hospital bed in the then bedroom,
once dining room, where you had at one time only celebrated.

The next morning he no longer resembled the man you had wed.

When the gurney took your Love out the door, you sat before the monitor, stunned, and alerted all you knew through the only words you had left.

Going Hungry

You sacrifice your grief like a meatball,
the last one, to your daughter, four,
who is still hungry - needing more

Most of the Days of the Week

On Monday you make pancakes, pay the bills, clean the floor, wipe down the counters, and begin chopping vegetables for soup. As the knife slices the onion thin, you peel away its outer layer and consider committing seppuku at noon.

On Tuesday you start the Crock-Pot, dust the blinds, rake the leaves, strip the beds, and carry the laundry downstairs. You put the wash on delicate, cold, and as you turn to go upstairs to the hum of the washer balancing its own mind, you longingly consider freshly washed, warmed, and crisp sheets tied gracefully around a rafter and your neck. Those beams appear strong.

Wednesday after tucking the kids into bed and starting the dishwasher, you wash your face, brush and floss your teeth, and line every pill bottle in the medicine cabinet up on the bathroom counter before considering what they will find in the morning. Then you carefully place the bottles back in the cupboard, turn out the lights, and climb into bed yourself, after checking the breaths of your children.

Thursday night you have a little bit too much to drink. Some wine. Several beers. Rum in a hot cup of tea. Then you remember something Nietzsche said about thoughts of suicide getting many through a dark night. This week you've made it three and a half days but it isn't the weekend yet. You aren't sure if N is right, but you know you can't drink the antifreeze.

Friday you go out for groceries and consider high speed, a curve, a tree, or maybe that bridge over there. But you probably wouldn't even be successful and then what a mess you'd make. No one would be there to clean it up. And the kids. Who would make them breakfast?

Saturday, you roll over to turn off the alarm but there isn't one. A blessing. Shortly thereafter there are kids on top of you, climbing over you, giggling, offering to get you coffee, begging for eggs and bacon, and so you make your way to the kitchen.

When the grease in the bacon pan begins to sizzle, you don't imagine dousing yourself in it or starting a grease fire. Instead you serve up breakfast and sip your coffee admiring the life you have created, the one still in the making.

When a leaf blowing in the wind seems like a hello.

I smoke my cigarette in the cold
staring up at a sky littered with stars
and talk to you about the kids, your stocking
hanging on the mantle,
Another holiday come while you've been
gone, another year survived without you.
I know I should be breathing in your scent
instead of the soot and nicotine, I
apologize for being far less than
I hope to be, but remind you that I baked your
favorite cookies, that while my ass is bigger,
my heart is too, it expands and expands,
filled to near-bursting with longing, and
when I exhale the last puff of peace, these
ten minutes visiting you in my mind, alone, here, shivering,
a speck on the planet talking to what specks of you are left, but also
to no one since we both know full well your ashes are ten feet
away in the other direction, through two layers of glass,
holding forth in a cabinet, a sudden rustle of leaves blows
my way and I peer down at the driveway and spontaneously
blow out, "hello," and the largest of the group raises its head,
or seems to, and waves.
And again, I say hello. And I pretend you hear.

How Contentment Comes

In the quiet of a Sunday morning when with covers over my head the children play quietly while I sleep until ten, I wake completely before joining them, making myself a double espresso bedside before journeying to their needs. Upon making breakfast, a poem surprise discovered in yesterday's pile of mail greets, and reading quietly to myself, my mind awakens to words and to thoughts rising to the unsoiled newness of late sun and of day sounds like bacon and laughter. I have not yet had to do anything in these early moments that I did not want to do, and there was no suffering in any of it. I may be able to ride on these brevities all of my life.

Bartering in MI

Sometimes you barter a trombone for a pick-up.
Sometimes it's a fixed vacuum for a six-pack.
We barter in any relationship.

I bartered with you. Two kids. A dog.
One dead husband; two ex-husbands.
You, one ex-wife; a few girlfriends.

When a six-pack is equal to a fixed vacuum,
you are good to go.

Love Begets Love

The night my mother died,
neither the man I'd recently slept with,
nor the one before who had given me a ring,
answered the phone.

The one who showed at her funeral,
I hadn't dated in four years.
He was happily betrothed to another.

But this time, you,
you were there.

Holding the children's hands,
inciting a pillow fight,
rubbing the small of my back,
holding my sobs close to your chest as I wept.

But that's not the story I want to tell.

I want to write about your curves.

When I first held you,
I couldn't help but compare,
Larger hands, slightly less hair there,
a lot more there, slenderer, quieter.

You, not him.

I compared you,
unfairly, of course, as one does.

But now I have gained a new voice singing,
a new voice singing, whistling, rather
a new life signaling life,
an urging forward.

Love begets love
Loss begets loss

But in this moment, now,
your curves,
the supple texture of your back,
your breath warming my cheeks.

Outside In

Sometimes I look inside my house and wonder who lives there—

Paintings on the walls, books lining the shelves, a dimly lit chandelier hovering above a single lit candle on the dining room table

Once I pulled into the drive and there was a boy leaning forward to light the candle, a girl setting the table, a man at the sink—a painting exhibiting chiaroscuro

No one else peering in would know this father had just entered the scene, that the girl as nightmares that the boy has nestled and locked a hidden place that recalls his father's deathbed breaths

What brush strokes captured the scene best, or at all, and what would be revealed should the frame change, should some of the paint be scraped away to reveal the original strokes, and more simply, how the mother about to arrive down center would present?

That evening observing the peaceful scene, the cold outside holding me in place, the warmth inside beckoning, the dog nudged me just as I was entering the stage of hopeful dreaming

Doorbell Advised

In aisle five they sell wireless doorbells with a
150-foot range—battery life 3 years for chime,
2 years for buttons for your new home, in this
old house, so your husband waits while your
legs take you to the world to get one
It had never before occurred to either of you that you would
need one, the old one rang just fine, for the house,
it wasn't until ten years into the marriage that his
muscles began failing, and not long after that the glass bell could
no longer be rung with a twist of his wrist that it was advised
Upon your return, your own wrist deftly
maneuvers with a knife the relentless plastic
packaging, freeing the two buttons and the
receiver you hope will save you both from
fear and further incapacitation
You have a dozen choices for chimes:
foghorn, steam engine, church bell,
the buzzer that sounds on a
game show answer
gone wrong
Last time he cried out for you, you were upstairs,
crying into the phone, you didn't hear him, not at
first, and then you did, and there he was,
down those many stairs and through the kitchen,
straddling the tub, having begun to
fall when he turned from the john, having
caught himself between the legs ten minutes
before, and still unable to get up
You hadn't known. You hadn't heard
—his voice having already grown faint
Now when the foghorn blows, you are assured you will
descend, you will right him when he tips, or falls
between the bed and the wall,
again, you will remain his loving sentinel, you will
cradle what remains of all 200 pounds of him,
folded into you the way he has before folded
all three of you into his chest

Until the day he cannot ring

First the depression of the button asking too much, and then
life itself, and the silenced buttons and this
receiver are put away in his drawer, in the
bedside table on his side of now
only your bed
And once you move to where the children will learn to play
again, one button will be placed in the kitchen, and another
next to your new marriage bed, in an again new home, with a
new husband, and you will ring the children instead,
and they will respond in harmony with gleeful anticipation
foghorn, steam engine, church bell, the buzzer that sounds on all
game shows gone wrong—and only you will
bear the difference, and shudder from the ignorance of
just how long these new batteries can
last

The Height of Gladness

I breathe you in, what's left of you, the oils from your skin still wrinkling these smooth sheets, balled up in a dusty closet, sleeping in the dark.

Your ashes were taken to the dump the day before yesterday, (the garbage men don't know).

Your books still line the shelves, the lines you wrote at dawn, singing to yourself.

You hummed off the road and into a dream, the minced meat still on your tongue, while I, opera-soaked, walked myself into a corner, and got hung up on a rack. The peace plant died two weeks ago, the one brought by Lucifer and his side-kick Jezebel, its last blossom a burnt sliver of a pod clinging clay-side.

I sit in the corner, imbibing to the last, and imagine you whole.

When I go, ashes to ashes, front to back, closed in on myself like a folded sheet of paper, spread me out, iron me, crease me, but no hospital corners, no, not for me.

Roll me in crackers so that the birds believe they are dining at the Ritz, then shove me off a precipice at the height of gladness.

Phantom Limbs

I tell my son each family has a tree.
I pencil lines on a page leading to his father, his sister, me:
"People, like trees, have branches."

Branches in our tree bow abruptly on one side:
One cracked unceremoniously—it was brittle—
Two committed suicide—snapping off willfully—
Another was in slow decay and was whittled away…
in each, the bark exposed the core.

I know, but do not tell.

I also recall, slowly, with lead, how else it is done:
other boughs break, peeling, cracking, succumbing—
only one splintered edge at a time.

On one side of my hand-drawn sketch,
the angled and slanted lines extend only toward absence—
one generation back from the boy, and the whole already recedes,
inching ringless, limbless, toward a well-known cliff.

Completing the halved tree, I tell my son, as I gesture in his direction:
"All families have trees—this one is yours—."

Spilling forth

Do you ever feel like the ideas are
spilling out of you,
pouring out of you,
like if you could do it over
and over
and over
you might be an architect
and create walls
or a plumber
and drain sewage
or maybe you would race
not on tracks going in circles but far, far away?

But instead you close your eyes and drink in the sounds of babies
and of love.

You recall the tingling sensations of lips, the scents of the unknown,
and you know it's for the love of the thing, not for how far it takes you
away from, or
closer to
yourself, but how far you can stretch
without breaking
that matters
that becomes a sort of profession,
I mean
confession
held

Dear,

In Memoriam

Sometimes the worst thing that can happen
is the thing that already has

When the worst thing that can happen
does happen, you think, "The decks are cleared,"
but they're not.

There is a worse thing,
always a worse thing.

Rather than anticipate its arrival
or recall the last quake—

Stir, stir the soup.
Light the candle.
Wash your face.

Call your mother, your wife, your daughter, the neighbor.

Call the one or two you've got left.

Then eat.

Author's Note

I am grateful to the editors of the journals where these poems first appeared and to the poets and poetry workshop participants of the 2017 summer Antioch Writers' Workshop for their insights and suggestions. I am thankful for the various professional and financial support of the English, Literature, and World Languages Department, the College of Arts & Sciences, and the Junior Faculty Fellows Program of the Faculty Center for Teaching and Learning at Ferris State University. I also very much appreciate the confidence of The College English Association and the South Atlantic Modern Language Association for offering opportunities to present a number of these poems at conferences. For my poetry education, I am indebted to forbears and friends in words, teachings, and deeds, especially my late father, poet Frank Fagan. Appreciation is also extended to my much-missed Illinois writing circle and my very spread about but forever writing tribe for encouragement, wit, and enlightenment. Deeply felt thanks to my dear friend and colleague, artist Carrie Weis, for gracing the cover with her beautiful artwork.

Deirdre Fagan is a widow, wife, mother of two, and writer of poetry, fiction, nonfiction, essays on literary criticism and pedagogy, and reference works. Fagan holds a master's in English and a doctorate in Humanistic Studies (English and Philosophy) from University at Albany, and a bachelor's in English from University at Buffalo.

She is the author of the book *Critical Companion to Robert Frost* and the articles, "Kay Ryan and Poetic Play," published in the *CEA Critic*, and "Emily Dickinson's Unutterable Word," published in the *Emily Dickinson Journal* and collected in *Bloom's Modern Critical Views: Emily Dickinson*, among others.

Her academic and creative work is available in print and online journals and collections, and she regularly presents at national and regional conferences. Her poem, "Outside In," was a finalist for Best of the Net 2018, and her poem, "Homesick," was nominated for a 2018 Pushcart. Fagan is a native New Yorker who has previously lived in Arizona, Florida, Illinois, and Maryland. She currently resides in Michigan where she is associate professor and coordinator of creative writing and Literature in Person in the English, Literature, and World Languages Department at Ferris State University. Fagan teaches creative writing, composition, poetry, and American literature. Meet her at deirdrefagan.com.

www.ingramcontent.com/pod-product-compliance
Lightning Source LLC
LaVergne TN
LVHW041507070426
835507LV00012B/1379